1

Abraham Lincoln's Republican Party knew they needed to preserve voting rights and enshrine it into law. After a much heated debate in Congress, they drafted the 15th Amendment: Declaring that the *right of citizens of the United States to vote shall not be denied or abridged by the United States or by any state on account of race, color, or previous condition of servitude.*

THE BOTCHED AMENDMENT

There are 27 amendments to the US constitution. While the 13th, 14, and 15th amendments are part and parcel of this US structure. The 15th amendment seems to be the one that is always being tugged at. And in a sense *botched,* by those attempting to suppress the Black vote. It is like giving something to someone, and after a feeling, based on your preconceived notions, you feel they do not deserve it.

You are threatened by their God-given potential to orchestrate and dominate. So, you place road-blocks endeavoring to keep them sitting on the fence. In your eyes on the sidelines is where they belong. So, to shred the constitution, you engage in tactical pursuits to deny them the rights of that endowment.

Black Americans awarded the right to vote over 150 years ago, but voter suppression still is an existential dilemma in the United States. We find it marinated and infesting cities and states wherever the black vote threatens the outcome of an election. Recent signs of its infestation were notable in the 2018 mid-term elections in Georgia, where long lines, reports of broken machines, and absentee ballots which were allegedly not counted.

Allan Lichtman, an American University history professor and author, Explains how the lack of a national voting right continues plaguing Americans today.

THE BOTCHED AMENDMENT

SUPPRESSING
THE BLACK VOTE

LIBERTY & JUSTICE

International Bestselling Author

John A. Andrews

Copyright © 2020 by John A. Andrews.
All rights reserved. Written permission must be
secured from the publisher to use or reproduce any
part of this book, except for brief quotations in
critical reviews or articles.

Published in the U.S.A. by
Books That Will Enhance Your Life™
A L I – Andrews Leadership International
www.JohnAAndrews.com
Cover Design: John A. Andrews
Cover Graphic Designer: A L I
Cover Photo: Aussie Active
Edited by:A L I
ISBN: **9798636595601**

THE BOTCHED AMENDMENT

TABLE OF CONTENTS

"Recent voting initiatives, such as stricter photo ID requirements, *poll-closures*, and *early-voting* cutbacks.
Have *disproportionately* impacted minority communities,"
Lichtman states.

The widespread debates over the 15th Amendment and the vision of mail-in-ballots are incredibly relevant today. A considerable segment of our populous who are eligible to vote would vote if convenient to do so—for example, the 80-year-old grandma who is bedridden and confined to stay-at-home. Let us call her Betsy.

Her husband died fighting for our country. They produced no kid, as he was deployed soon after their marriage. She remained devoted to him in life as well as in death. Betsy worked as a Librarian for over 40 years. Also, she served as a deaconess at her local church. Stricken with arthritis and other related diseases, she has become confined to her bedroom.

Yet, every week she sends her tithe and offerings to the church. Her pension, plus her husband, is a decent sum combined. With her reading glasses on, she writes the check, licks and seals the envelope, affix a stamp and mailed to the church.

Betsy has seen better days and would like to cast her vote if provided with a ballot. This story is an extreme scenario, but I have decided to take the voting process out on a limb.

Why should Betsy be denied her right to participate in our democratic process?

2

States like Oregon, Arizona, California, District of Columbia, Hawaii, Montana, Nevada, New Jersey, and Utah have been using this system. Some of these states for more than a decade.

This solution to make elections innocuous, accessible, and timely is now readily available whether the coronavirus pandemic lingers until the general election in November or not. Whether we are at war - Whether a natural disaster emerges, this proven solution also makes all votes easier for voters to participate. It boosts turnout. It is cheaper to administer. It is more secure - mailed-out paper ballots are not only virus-proof. They are suppression-proof – everyone who wants to vote can do so. It is cyber-proof too – goodbye Russia.

In the case of Oregonians: They have been happily voting by mail for almost two decades, and Oregon Senator Ron Wyden has introduced legislation with Senator Amy Klobuchar of Minnesota to advance the nation toward that move.

On Tuesday, April 7, Wisconsin voters risked possible infection at the polls after the State's highest court rejected Democratic Gov. Tony Evers' late-in-the-game moves to postpone the primary. Coincidently, on the eve the Wisconsin primary. News surfaced that Blacks were the highest percentage of deaths from the coronavirus, aka COVID-19. Milwaukee happens to be the Blackest populated city in that state.

Wisconsin's press to the polls offers a test case of what happens when fears of the coronavirus or other catastrophes clash with primary elections. This primary election during the coronavirus pandemic proceeded as scheduled despite State-Democrats' attempts to move it and extend absentee voting. The event occurred despite a stay-in-place order, which requires the state's residents to stay at home to prevent further spread of the virus, which has been a menace to the United States—branding the country as the historic center for demises.

Voting rights advocates feared that the decision to hold in-person voting on Tuesday could put People's health at risk and disenfranchise voters. On Monday, late in the day, The US Supreme Court overturned a lower court ruling that allowed absentee ballots to arrive late - until April, 13th.

Such a decision not only thrust a yank in the steering wheel of the health system but put voters at a disadvantage. Voters, who because of their constitutional right to vote. They showed up at inadequately crewed polling stations despite social distancing. Additionally, voting rights advocates warned of this catastrophe and echoed: *The primary remained plagued with long lines and closed polling location lead to a suppressed voter turnout.*

This pandemic, which originated in Wuhan, China in late 2019, knows no race, class, or gender. It attacks like a whirlwind anyone in its path. However, if you are unable to elude it, it has won the battle.

According to sources: at least 70% of deaths from COVID-19 in Louisiana and occupy a high percentage in other states. With blacks working in the mostly service-oriented jobs, the death toll on the ethnicity climbs.

Allegedly, factors influencing this high mortality rate among blacks in this pandemic is not only concerning but demands scrutiny:

- Blacks hold most of the jobs on the front lines.
- Blacks are the most underserved people.
- Blacks have limited access to Health Care.
- Plus, Blacks always get disfranchised.
- Testing, in most cases, could be cost-effective for most blacks.

Most coronavirus testings get done in Suburban America instead of Urban America.

3

Back in 2016, before the general election, in Wisconsin, a federal judge found that the state's restrictive voter ID law led to *real incidents of disenfranchisement, which undermine rather than enhance confidence in elections, particularly in minority communities*. While there was no evidence of widespread voter fraud in Wisconsin, found that the law was *a cure worse than the disease.*

Wisconsin, in addition to imposing strict voter ID requirements, the law cut back on early voting, required people to live in an area for at least 28 days before voting, and prohibited emailing absentee ballots to voters.

Back in 2019, presiding circuit court Judge Paul V. Malloy of Ozaukee County, Wisconsin, removed 234,000 voters from the statewide rolls. He was ruling that state law compelled him to do so.

A study conducted by Priorities USA, a progressive advocacy group, estimated that strict ID laws in Wisconsin led to a significant decrease in voter turnout in 2016, with a disproportionate effect on African-American and Democratic-leaning voters.

In this 2020 primary, More than 50,000 voters had expected to vote in Milwaukee, the state's largest city, but the number of polling locations was reduced from more than 180 to just 5, according to The New York Times. Thereby creating long lines of voters spread out for blocks as they attempted to practice social distancing. Some voters were waiting for more than two hours, according to the NYT. One voter, a nurse, rushed from work to cast her ballot. According to her statement: "I got there 3 minutes late, and the polling station was closed". No one bothered to accommodate her right to a vote. Her delay, no doubt due to her battling the pandemic on the frontlines.

Molly McGrath, a voting rights campaign strategist with the American Civil Liberties Union, told Business Insider that: Tuesday's primary in Wisconsin was like *voter suppression on steroids.*

McGrath continued:

"The bottom line is no one should have to choose between protecting their health and protecting their right to vote."

Depicting long lines of Black and Brown voters waiting to cast ballots. McGrath further elaborated:

"A lot of the same communities and the same people who are impacted by voter suppression. Are now impacted in this pandemic."

Meanwhile, Jay Heck, executive director of Common Cause Wisconsin said in a statement:

"Wisconsin's absentee ballot rules are no doubt disenfranchising voters." As in the case of the nurse and many other would-be-voters.

Seasoned politicians knowledgeable of the voting debacle are now advocating how much Democrats need to avoid what happened in Wisconsin - not returning in the November election.

Due to the COVID-19 pandemic, fifteen states nationwide, Alaska, Connecticut, Delaware, Georgia, Hawaii, Indiana, Kentucky, Louisiana, Maryland, New York, Ohio, Pennsylvania, Rhode Island, West Virginia, Wyoming - and the territory of Puerto Rico have pushed back their primary election.

Wisconsin remains mounted on the voter suppression radar.

4

The fight between America's 45th President Donald Trump and Congress is now brewing regarding mail-in-ballots. Trump claiming voter fraud would occur. However, there has been no proof of such. While Congress has already approved some $40 Billion in the recent $2 Trillion packages. In part destined to harden the US voting structure. A showdown between

Congress and POTUS over mail-in-ballots seems imminently protracted.

Ali Lozano, a voting rights outreach coordinator at the Texas Civil Rights Project, said she is continually fighting against intrusion into the 15th Amendment and 1965 Voting Rights Act in Texas, *from voter purge lists to racial gerrymandering to voter intimidation at the polls.*

"I consider it an aspirational law,"

Lozano said of the 15th Amendment.

"People need to be aware there is a difference between passage and implementation. There is a question about how these policies are implemented. Plus, are they doing what they're intended to do?"

While Jill Savitt, president and chief executive of the National Center for Civil and Human Rights in Atlanta, claimed the 15th Amendment's significance is "enormous," *given all the blood, shed to adopt the amendment.*

While the death toll continues, and blacks remain a high percentage in the US casualties. There is no public data available on COVID-19 cases by race, a pattern of over-representation by black Americans has emerged in states or jurisdictions that are sharing race-based numbers.

Experts reiterate, *blacks are disproportionately impacted by underlying health conditions linked to poverty, face discrimination in medical care, and are more likely to work jobs that require them to leave their homes.* For example, in New York City, most blacks commute to and from work using the mass transit system and local city buses - a communal transportation environment where social-distancing proves problematic, especially during rush hours.

The Nation's top doctor, Surgeon General Jerome Adams who is black, told CBS News on April 7:

"We know that blacks are more likely to have diabetes, heart disease, lung disease,"

These chronic illnesses, which are, in turn, linked to poverty and structural racism, can lead to more severe forms of the COVID-19 disease.

Adams, who is himself black and has high blood pressure and asthma, added:

"I represent that legacy of growing up poor and black in America… And I, and many black Americans, are at higher risk for COVID." - Emerging trend.

By the way, days later, he spoke at a White House Coronavirus Taskforce briefing where he displayed his asthmatic inhaler, a crutch he has used since childhood.

However, it is a given that blacks are continually dying from coronavirus twice the rate of white Americans. At the same time, Urban Americans and not Suburban Americans get disenfranchised when it comes to testing.

5

The tactic of voter suppression in the United States dates back to 1877 when the Dixiecrats began to impose a series of laws designed to suppress the black vote. The measure intended to prevent eligible voters from exercising their right to vote. Since then, there have been numerous and varied efforts to disenfranchise blacks who are likely to vote.

Fast forward to 1998, Florida, the Country's most southern state created the Florida Central Voter File to combat vote fraud documented in the 1997 Miami mayoral election. As a result, many people got purged from voter registration lists there. Mainly because their names were similar to those of other convicted felons. Criminals were not permitted to vote at that time under Florida law. According to the *Palm Beach Post*, African-Americans accounted for 88% of those removed from the rolls but were only about 11% of Florida's voters.

However, according to the Florida Department of Law Enforcement, nearly 89% of felons convicted in Florida are black. Therefore, a purge of convicted criminals could include a disproportionately high number of blacks.

The *Post* supplemented: "a review of state records, internal emails of DBT employees and testimony before the civil rights commission and an election task force showed no evidence that minorities got specifically targeted".

Relatedly, during 2008, more than 98,000 registered Georgia voters got removed from the roll of voters because of a computer glitch. They were described as a mismatch in their personal identification information. At least 4,500 voters had to prove their citizenship later to regain their right to vote.

Additionally, Georgia got challenged for requesting Social Security records for verification checks on about 2 million voters. That was more requests than any other state underwent. This got challenged in court, and an attorney involved in the lawsuit said Georgia violated a federal law prohibiting widespread voter purges within 90 days of an election. Thereby, contending that the letters were sent out too close to the election date. To which the director of the American Civil Liberty Union's Georgia Voting Rights Project said, "They are systematically using these lists and matching them and using those matches to send these letters out to voters."

He added:

"They are using a systematic purging procedure that is expressly prohibited by federal laws if appropriately eligible people are getting challenged and purged.

Meanwhile, Elise Shore, a regional attorney for the Mexican American Legal Defense and Educational Fund (MALDEF), agreed the letters appear to violate two federal laws against voter purging within 90 days of the election.

"People are getting targeted, and people are being told they are noncitizens. Including both naturalized citizens and U.S.-born citizens," She said. "They are told they are not eligible to vote, based on information in a database that had not been checked and approved by the Department of Justice (DOJ), and that we know has flaws in it."

Shore further elaborated.

Subsequently, Secretary of State Karen Handel denied that the removal of voters' names was an instance of voter suppression.

Meanwhile, in New York between November 2015 and early 2016, over 120,000 voters were dropped from rolls in Brooklyn. New York Officials in defense have stated that the purge was a mistake and that those cut represented a "broad cross-section" of the electorate.

Nevertheless, a WNYC investigation found that the purge had disproportionately affected majority-Hispanic districts. The board then announced that it would reinstate all voters in time for the 2016 congressional primary.

Consequently, the Board of Elections subsequently suspended the Republican appointee in connection to the purge but retained her Democratic counterpart.

Limitations on early and absentee voting have emerged as a wrench in the toolbox designed to suppress black votes.

Reportedly, a few years ago in North Carolina, Republican lawmakers requested data on various voting practices, broken down by race. They then structurally passed laws that restricted voting and registration. These acts got orchestrated in many ways that disproportionately affected African Americans. This strategy included cutting back on early voting. In a 2016 appellate court case, the U.S. Court of Appeals for the Fourth Circuit struck down a law that removed the first week of early voting. The court disputed that the GOP used the data they gathered to remove the first week of early voting because more African American voters to circumvent their tactics voted during that week. African Americans it has been discovered are more likely to vote for Democrats.

Between 2008 and 2012 in North Carolina, at least 70% of African American voters voted early. Some did so on Sundays before or after their church services. When cuts to early voting emerged, African American turnout in early voting plummeted by 8.7%, equating to around 66,000 votes in that state.

The 2018 gubernatorial candidate Stacy Abrams of Georgia shared a story of an 18-year-old Georgian Who Says She Had Trouble Voting on Election Day.

Reportedly, the race for Governor of Georgia had not yet materialized. Democratic candidate Stacey Abrams vowed to fight, ensuring every single vote got counted. Abrams is also using her Instagram page to share stories of Georgians, who had trouble voting on Election Day.

One of the Georgians highlighted by the gubernatorial hopeful is JaKayla, a freshman at Albany State University. The university is in Dougherty County; the Abrams campaign launched a legal challenge revolving around this very same county due to what Abrams claims is the mishandling of its absentee ballots.

JaKayla did not speak about the suit but claimed she and her fellow students had an enormous amount of trouble voting on November, 6th. Other students faced similar difficulty according to the first-time voter:

"This was my first time voting,"

JaKayla wrote.

"I wanted to vote early, but as a student without a car, I was told to wait because there would be a polling place on campus on Election Day. When I went to vote on Election Day, I was told I had to vote by 'provisional ballot' – then I found out that there were two polling locations on the campus. I asked if I needed to go to the other polling place to vote and was told, 'NO.' I just needed to fill out a provisional ballot."

The freshman wanted to cast a real ballot and contacted the secretary of state's office, which, at that time, was led by Abrams' rival, GOP gubernatorial candidate Brian Kemp.

Officials allegedly told JaKayla they didn't know why she wasn't being allowed to cast an ordinary ballot.

7

The State of Georgia has an affinity with policing black citizens who dare to vote. Reportedly, in 2010, when African Americans in Brooks county organized a massive get-up-and-vote turn-out to elect the first majority-black school board in its history, then secretary of State, Brian Kemp, became antsy. He orchestrated and had a dozen African American activists and school board members arrested.

Like a snail, this dilemma dragged through the courts for almost 5 years. Ending up, on the side of the law there were no convictions for voter fraud. However, there remained a lancing effect as life got disrupted, jobs lost, and the venom for voting marinated and festered.

After the 2018 mid-term election which got delayed for a gubernatorial result in Georgia, Senator Cory Booker a Democrat from New jersey echoed:

"There should be a federal investigation. The Justice Department should be investigating that election to make sure it was fair and the decisions were not to advantage someone politically, but to protect voters and the voting process,"

He told Yahoo.

Booker was adamant about wanting the U.S. Department of Justice to investigate the controversial election. Although he admitted, he has "not been in the weeds" with the latest news about the election. Nevertheless, but he did not shy away from demanding justice for Abrams.

"I think that Stacey Abrams' election is being stolen from her, using what I think are insidious measures to disenfranchise certain groups of people."

He further elaborated.

Abrams got interlocked in a that close gubernatorial race in Georgia. Her Republican rival, Brian Kemp, unorthodoxly oversaw the election as secretary of State. This was problematic from the start of the campaign and frankly pre-campaign. Several issues, including long waits at the polls, were reported on

Election Day. Evident by the story shared earlier by Abrams regarding 18-year-old voter JaKayla.

MULTIPLE LAWSUITS got filed to ensure integrity even after those polls were closed, and the vote got tallied for weeks. At stake were all absentee and provisional ballots uncounted.

In addition to multiple lawsuits, there was pushback from the Kemp camp.

"Since election night, hardworking Georgians have watched how the 'new' Democratic Party behaves," Cody Hall, Kemp's press secretary vented.

"Stacey Abrams and her radical backers will stop at nothing to undermine democracy and attempt to steal this election to be Georgia's next governor."

She continued.

Abrams' campaign counter-pushed-back against this narrative and accused the office of the secretary of State of deceiving voters.

Meanwhile, the date for vote certification got pushed back, and a federal judge ordered roughly 1,000 absentee ballots that gotten rejected to get included in official vote tallies.

"The Trump Justice Department should investigate what happened," Booker echoed. "That is not just the appearance of impropriety. To me, it is the appearance of voter fraud, voter disenfranchisement, voter suppression."

No help came from the DOJ in that matter.

Meanwhile, Senator Sherrod, a Democrat from Ohio, weighed in, according to NBC News.

"If Stacey Abrams does not win in Georgia, they stole it," Brown said one day after Georgia authorities were supposed to begin recounting those votes. "It is clear. It is clear. I say that publicly, and it is clear."

Brown brought up gerrymandering and voter suppression targeting people of color while speaking at that National Action Network conference.

"Republicans win elections by redistricting and reapportionment and voter suppression and all the ways they try to scare people, particularly people of color," he added.

Lauren Groh-Wargo, Abrams' campaign manager, said during the vote debacle:

"The secretary of State office is lying about the number of votes cast. As well as the number of votes - Still to be counted. How do we know? We went to the counties directly to see the votes and count them for ourselves."

Coincidentally, Kemp resigned from his secretary of state post after the November 6 elections. Abrams refused to concede and continued to fight to have every ballot counted. A very contentious election that still leaves unanswered questions regarding the suppressing of the black vote.

Abrams is still in the fight for election reform in Georgia even though Kemps now occupies the state office as governor.

It seems like Georgia has no respect for the 15th amendment and time and time again endeavors to keep blacks at bay. In Louisville, Georgia, in October 2018, Black senior citizens were told to get off a bus that was to have taken them to a polling place for early voting.

This bus trip was supposed to have been part of the

"South Rising" bus tour sponsored by the advocacy group Black Voters Matter. A clerk of the local Jefferson County Commission allegedly called the intended voters' senior center to claim that the bus tour constituted "political activity," which gets barred at events sponsored by the county. How fitting?

Latosha Brown, one of the founders of Black Voters Matter, smelled some smoke and described the trip's prevention as a clear-cut case of "...voter intimidation. That is voter suppression, Southern style."

She echoed.

The NAACP Legal Defense and Educational Fund sent a letter to the county calling for an "immediate investigation" into the incident, which it condemned as "an unacceptable act of voter intimidation," that "potentially violates several laws."

Georgia's Secretary of State, Brian Kemp, the Republican gubernatorial nominee, was the official in charge of determining whether or not voters will be allowed to vote in the November 2018 election and has been accused of voter suppression. How convenient for anti-democracy?

Minority voters are statistically more likely to have names that contain hyphens, suffixes, or other punctuation that can make it more challenging to match their names in databases, experts noted. Plus, they and are more likely to have their voter applications suspended by Kemp's office.

Reportedly, Barry C. Burden, a professor at the University of Wisconsin-Madison and director of its Elections Research Center said,

"An unrealistic rule of this sort will falsely flag many legitimate registration forms. Moreover, the evidence indicates that minority residents are more likely to be flagged than are whites."

Kemp has suspended the applications of 53,000 voters, a majority of whom are minorities believed to be in the hyphenated name category. Additionally, Strict voter registration deadlines in Georgia prevented 87,000 Georgians from voting because they had registered after the period.

Said Charles Stewart III, Professor of Political Science at Massachusetts Institute of Technology:

Even if everyone who is on a pending list is eventually allowed to vote, it places more hurdles in the way of those voters on the list, who are disproportionately black and Hispanic.

9

It was leading up to the 2010 Maryland gubernatorial election the campaign of Republican candidate Bob Ehrlich hired a consultant who advised that "the first and most desired outcome is voter suppression." It was all or nothing. They plotted to *have African-American voters stay home*. To carry out this feat, the Republicans placed thousands of Election Day robocalls to Democratic voters, telling them that the Democratic candidate, Martin O'Malley, had won. Although factually, the polls were still open for two more hours.

The Republicans' call, got worded to seem as if it came from Democrats. Reportedly, the voters got notified: "Relax. Everything is fine. The only thing left is to watch it on TV tonight." The calls reached 112,000 voters in majority-African American areas. They bought into the hype.

As a result, in 2011, Ehrlich's campaign manager, Paul Schurick, was convicted of fraud and other charges because of those calls. Consequently, in 2012, he was sentenced to 30 days of home detention, a one-year suspended jail sentence, and 500 hours of community service over the four years of his probation and no fine or jail time. Fortunately, the Democratic candidate won by a margin of more than 10 percent.

FAST FORWARD, in 2015, early voting controversy in spiraled Maryland. In Maryland's Montgomery County, Republicans planned to move two early-voting sites from densely populated Bethesda and Burtonsville to more sparsely populated areas in Brookville and Potomac.

To camouflage the deal, they claimed to be aiming for more "geographic diversity". Caught with a hand inside the cookie jar, Democrats aggressively accused them of trying to suppress the vote. This Burtonsville site had the most minority voters of all the early-voting sites in the county. At the same time, the proposed new locations were in more suburban and Republican-friendly with fewer minority residents. The Republican election board chairman admitted at a County Council committee that he and two GOP colleagues held a conference call with the chairman of Montgomery's Republican Party Central Committee. Was this a perfect call?

Todd Eberly, a political science professor from Saint Mary's College, called the claim by the Republicans, *a stupid defense*.

They said the call, from which Democrats were excluded, was legal. Democrats called it a violation of Maryland's Open Meetings Act.

10

President Trump said that if the United States switched to all-mail voting, "you would never have a Republican elected in this country again." Pundits say for the first time, he is right about something. Such a decision will ultimately validate the 15th Amendment – putting an end to suppressing the Black Vote.

According to reports: The G.O.P. speaker of the House in Georgia said an all-mail election would be "extremely devastating to Republicans."

While Representative Thomas Massie, a Kentucky Republican, said universal mail voting would be "the end of our republic as we know it."

Meanwhile, pundits who have studied voting by mail begged to differ.

False claims by Republicans about vote-by-mail fraud, prevails. While there is no evidence to back up their argument, that all-mail elections favor Democrats. However, Mr. Trump and some of his allies from the right are warning vote-by-mail poses an existential threat to the Republican party. In hopes of galvanizing Republican opposition to a voting method viewed as safer than in-person voting in the era of the coronavirus.

The main argument by Mr. Trump and other Republicans is three-pronged and not in their favor:

1. Voting by mail is more accessible than going to the polls.
2. More people will vote if the process is easier
3. When more significant numbers of people vote, more will vote for Democrats.

In the states and counties that have transitioned to all-mail voting, there has been little evidence of partisan advantage for either side because of mail voting, according to Robert Stein, a Rice University professor who has helped put in place vote-by-mail systems.

Filling out a ballot at home also affords people more time to think about their vote. Dr. Stein found that voters spent about three and a half minutes when they went to a voting booth, but took about two days to complete a ballot they had received at home.

"Vote-by-mail has a way of affecting voter turnout in a way that we don't always think about," he said. "It increases turnout and attention for races that you would expect people would not vote for, like county judges and people you've never heard of."

Stein elaborates.

Before the coronavirus emerged as a global pandemic, Democrats had generally favored ways to expand access to voting by mail. Some senators have been working on creating bills since. While Republicans frequently argued in favor of tightening voter identification and registration requirements, claiming without evidence that easing restrictions invited voter fraud.

A 2013 study of voters in Washington by professors at Yale and the University of California, San Diego, found that voting by mail increased turnout by 2 to 4 percentage points, with low-participating voters more likely to be influenced than others.

Why not? Let's make it a level playing field. Every registered voter can participate in the process.

11

Vote by mail is not a complicated process. It's simple and a quickie. The state mails ballots to voters. The voters can fill them out comfortably in their homes. They then return the vote in the mail or bring it to a secure location of choice. This natural process can also be classified as Vote-at-home. Very convenient, as I've mentioned in the case of Betsy.

This process of voting could, by November 2020 or if not in a few months, become the new normal when it comes to voting. Our Country spent over $13 million for the 2016 Muller Investigation into our elections. Moving to Vote-By-Mail would eliminate the need to investigate cyber investigations and other related election interference.

Several states have already been using the process of Mail-In-Vote, while others are getting acclimated. Some participating states mail the ballots to all voters. Some mail to anyone who requests a Vote By Mail Ballot. The others will only send to voters who have an excuse for wanting a ballot in the mail.

Western states are championing, as indicated in the 2018 mid-term election. Reportedly, two-thirds of their voters used a mail-out-ballot. Colorado, Hawaii, Oregon, Utah, and Washington are five states which have already prepared to mail ballots to all registered voters.

These five states plus the District of Columbia let anyone request a ballot mailed to them every election: Arizona, California, Montana, Nevada, New Jersey, and DC. Just sign up for the process, and you are set. It is a win-win! If you reside in any of these states, you are set. Make sure they have the printing, mailing, and drop-off capacities to facilitate a likely surge in Vote By Mail ballots.

Meanwhile, at least 16 states because of jurisdictions logistics effectively utilize the ballot by mail process. Alaska, Arizona, California, Florida, Idaho, Kansas, Maryland, Minnesota, Missouri, Montana, Nebraska, Nevada, New Jersey, New Mexico, North Dakota, and Wyoming. While in Idaho, 21 of the 44 counties have at least one precinct that uses only mailed ballots.

In multiple states, any voter is allowed to request a vote by mail. However, they are required to re-request the ballot every election and annually.

There are at least 17 states that only let voters request Vote By Mail if they have an excuse. President Trump said he voted by mail in one of Florida's recent election. His apology could have been – being at the White house continually is a challenge to be there in person at this time if someone has an excuse as in the case of Betsy who's unable to come to the polling station. That's a great excuse.

As I've mentioned, Vote-by-Mail could soon become the new normal. So, do your homework and make your requests. In some cases, you may need to push your State in this decision. It is your right. Contact your Senator and Congressman and drive them. It is your right to request what you want, and voting is right and should not be inconvenient.

Until one is committed, there is hesitance, the chance to drawback. Always ineffectiveness. Concerning all acts of initiative (and creation), there is one elemental truth the ignorance of which kills countless ideas and splendid plans; that the moment one commits oneself, then providence moves too. All sorts of things occur to help one that would never have otherwise occurred. A whole stream of events issues from the decision, raising in one's favor all manner of unforeseen incidents and meetings and material assistance which no man could have dreamed would come his way. Whatever you can do or dream you can begin it. Genius has boldness and power and magic in it. Begin now.

- Goethe

12

Whenever I think of commitment, my mind goes back to the airplane taxiing down the runway scenario. Before take-off, the pilot receives the go-ahead from the air traffic control tower. He then engages the aircraft. It picks up speed, engages the sky, and the landing gear retracts as it becomes airborne.

As the aircraft gains altitude past 30,000 feet, passengers get instructed to unfasten their seatbelts -

refreshments get served. That plane became committed to fly. The pilot announces the estimated time of arrival and the weather in that city of destination. There is an end in mind.

A few years ago, I was at a business conference on the east coast and heard the keynote speaker share this story:

A very wealthy man bought a vast ranch in Arizona and invited some of his closest associates to see it. After touring the 1,500 acres of mountains, rivers, and grasslands, he took everybody to the house. The house was as spectacular as the scenery. In the back of the house was the largest swimming pool they had ever seen. However, it got filled with alligators. The owner explained:

"I value courage more than anything. It is what made me a billionaire. I value courage so much that if anyone dares to jump in that pool and swim to the other side, I will give them whatever they want, my land, my house, my money, anything."

Of course, everybody laughed at the challenge and turned to follow the owner into the house for lunch. Suddenly they heard a splash. Turning around, they saw a guy splashing and thrashing into the water, swimming for his life as the alligators swarmed after him. After

several death-defying seconds, the human-made it unharmed to the other side. The wealthy billionaire was amazed, but he stuck to his promise.
He said:
"You are a man of courage. You can have anything you want, house, money, land, etc., whatever you want is yours."
The swimmer, breathing heavily, looked up and said:
"I just want to know who pushed me in the pool."

-Unknown

Some examples of being pushed into action include the story of one Alabama seamstress:
One December evening in 1955, a seamstress for a department store in Montgomery, Alabama, boarded a city bus en-route to her home.
It was during the civil rights revolution when blacks were only legally permitted to sit at the back of a bus. She walked past the "whites only" section towards the middle of the bus.
With frequent stops, the bus filled up. The driver, a white man, noticed that more people of his race were still boarding. So, he ordered the people in the seamstress Rosa Parks' row to move to the back of the bus. They turned a deaf ear. Frustrated, he barked at

those black passengers. They all moved except for Rosa Parks.

Another story I once heard helps to put commitment into perspective:

One day a chicken and a pig were riding in a taxi. Simultaneously, they noticed a billboard displaying "The Great American breakfast" (bacon and eggs). The chicken looks across at the pig and remarks.

"Look at us up there! That is awesome, isn't it?"

The pig with no time to waste, responds:

"For you, it's all in a day's work, but for me, its total commitment."

The chicken was involved, but the pig got committed. We find that at times commitment could require all you've got.

In 1963, the late Dr. Martin Luther King Jr. while addressing a segment of the American populous echoed:

"If a man hasn't discovered something that he will die for, he isn't fit to live."

MLK's life was saturated with a cause greater than self. His cause required all or nothing.

13

Many Blacks shy away from the electoral process either as voters or volunteers. Why should I get involved? Some query. If time affords, it's great to know how the process works even on a volunteer basis. This upcoming election is not only a must vote for every American, but adequate staffing is going to be required more than any other election in this country's history.

Remember, "elections have consequences."

Experts agree we don't need to repeat the same bad experiences of the past, especially when it comes to the vote. *Getting out of the majority is paramount.*

Albert Einstein, the famous scientist, penned: *The definition of **insanity** is doing the same thing over and over and expecting different results.*

We ought to do whatever we can to make our election day a federal holiday. At the outset, expect a fight. There was a big one when MLK day got proposed as a holiday.

When government buildings, schools, and workplaces are required to close on Election Day. This frees up many more people who would be more inclined to vote. Currently, many voters have to rush from work, use their lunch break, or to catch the polling station before work. While for others, they have to facilitate voting between work and school. Commuting in densely populated cities could prove problematic. Rush hour traffic on a work-day is always a drag. For example, New York and Los Angeles. For people down to their last dime, voting and going to work become a toss-up.

Bills to support such a transition are already debated. Presidential candidate and Senator Bernie Sanders has introduced a bill that could push Election Day as "Democracy Day,"

While John Conyers, a former Michigan state representative, proposed legislation in 2016 to make Election Day a federal holiday. Supporting a bill is your civic right.

If there is an organization in your city that supports voter suppression, get involved immediately, and support. You can research these organizations online. If you cannot find a group and belong to a church, talk to your Bishop or Pastor regarding your involvement getting one started.

Stacey Abrams, the former gubernatorial candidate of Georgia, could be a great resource on this topic. Abrams no doubt hard to reach, but you can follow her on social media. This subject is very dear to her heart.

Some national organizations include VoteRiders. This organization resides in multiple states. They facilitate free voter ID resources & services for voters who need to obtain ID or who need information about what ID is required to vote in the United States.

Plus, any group set up to protect voting rights is a worthy cause not only for you but also for your posterity.

There is a high demand for workers at polling stations. If these facilities are staffed, voters showing up at the last moment could get to cast their vote. Represent! Represent! Represent!

Additionally, I have been made aware you can host a *voter registration drive.* Many celebrity artists have voters register as part of their concert tours while multiple websites provide information on the *How To's.*

Once again, your local church might be willing to assist in such a drive. There's also a 50 State Voter Registration Drive Guide online.

14

President Trump is pushing for a non-vote-by-mail in the upcoming general election as was discussed. His main concern or objection has to do with non-voter-ID. In 2013, the state House of North Carolina passed a bill that requires voters to show a photo ID issued by North Carolina, a passport, or a military identification card to begin in 2016. Out-of-state drivers' licenses were to be accepted only if the voter registered within 90 days of the election, and a university photo identification was not acceptable.

In July 2016, a three-judge panel of the Fourth Circuit Court of Appeals reversed a trial court decision in some consolidated actions. The Court struck down the law's photo ID requirement. Finding, that the new voting provisions targeted African Americans "with almost surgical precision." And that the legislators had acted with clear "discriminatory intent" in enacting strict election rules. Thus, shaping the rules based on data they received about African-American registration and voting patterns.

On May 15, 2017, the U.S. Supreme Court declined to review the Appeals Court ruling.

Coincidentally in that same month of 2017, Donald Trump established the Presidential Advisory Commission on Election Integrity, as rumor has it for preventing voter fraud. Critics have suggested its determination is voter suppression. The commission, then led by Kansas attorney general and Republican gubernatorial nominee Kris Kobach, a staunch advocate of strict voter ID laws and a proponent of the Crosscheck system.

Crosscheck is a national database designed to check for voters registered in more than one state by comparing names and dates of birth. Researchers at Stanford

University, the University of Pennsylvania, Harvard University, and Microsoft found that for every legitimate instance of double registration, it finds. Crosscheck's algorithm returns approximately 200 false positives. Consequently, Kobach has been repeatedly sued by the American Civil Liberties Union - ACLU and other civil rights organizations for trying to restrict voting rights in Kansas.

Reportedly, on February 20, 2016, while speaking to a committee of Kansas 2nd Congressional District delegates, regarding their challenges of the proof-of-citizenship voting law he championed in 2011, Kobach said:

"The ACLU and their fellow communist friends, the League of Women Voters — you can quote me on that, sued".

Often, voter fraud gets cited as a justification for such measures, even when the incidence of voter fraud is low.

Meanwhile, in Iowa, lawmakers passed a strict voter ID law with the potential to disenfranchise some 260,000 voters. Out of 1.6 million votes cast in Iowa in 2016, there were only 10 allegations of voter fraud; none were cases of impersonation that a voter ID law could have prevented according to reports.

Only one person, a Republican voter, was convicted. Iowa Secretary of State Paul Pate, the architect of the bill, admitted: "We've not experienced widespread voter fraud in Iowa."

15

Voting disinformation is another ploy used to conduct voter suppression among Blacks. This trickery procedure involves giving voters false information about when and how to vote, leading them to fail to cast valid ballots.

Reportedly, this occurred, for example, in recall elections for the Wisconsin State Senate in 2011. Americans for Prosperity, a conservative political advocacy group, founded in 2004 by brothers Charles and David Koch to support Republican candidates and causes in the United States. The duo is once known as the Koch Brothers. In 1980, David Koch ran as the Libertarian Party's vice-presidential candidate.

The Koch brothers sent many Democratic voters a mailing that gave an incorrect deadline for returning absentee ballots. Voters, who relied on the deadline in the mailing could have sent in their ballots too late for them to be counted. The organization later claimed that it was caused by a typographical error.

Just before the 2018 elections, *The New York Times* warned readers of numerous types of deliberate misinformation, sometimes targeting specific voter demographics. These types of disinformation included false information about casting ballots online by email and by text message, the circulation of doctored photographs in 2016, which claimed Immigration and Customs Enforcement *ICE* agents were arresting voters at polling places. They included threatening language meant to intimidate Latino voters. *Polling place hoaxes, disinformation on remote voting options, suspicious texts, voting machine malfunction rumors, misleading photos and videos, and false voter fraud allegations.*

The *Times* added: messages purportedly sent by Trump to voters in Indiana, Kansas, Michigan, and Georgia got disseminated from Republicans. In 2018,

Trump spread information about defective machines in a single Utah county, giving the impression that such difficulties were occurring nationwide.

16

Blacks consistently get targeted. This inappropriate action dated back to the pre-1960s and sparked the civil rights movement. In many states, this, unfortunately, remains a natural occurrence. Like waiting in Starbucks while black, sleeping at Yale while black, driving while black in addition to voting while black.

We find adequate black access to public spaces, such as the voting booth, activated, as noted by the federal - a targeting of African American voters. The targeting of African Americans was disproportionate in North Carolina after the US supreme court gutted the necessary protection of the Voting Rights Act in 2013. The substance for North Carolina's assault was evident: black people dared to access their 15th amendment rights.

Reportedly, since 2000, African American voter registration had increased by 51.1% in the state, and blacks also had a *higher voter turnout rate than white registered voters in both the 2008 and 2012 presidential elections.*

The state required ID's which its research showed a disproportionate number of black people did not have. And, the GOP slashed the number of early voting sites in Guilford County, which is nearly 30% African American, from "16 in 2012 to a single location" in 2016.

As a result, according to Think Progress Magazine, "turnout so far is down 85%".

There was duplicated elimination of early voting sites in Mecklenburg County, home to the city of Charlotte, and 15% of the state's African American population. Elated regarding what they had accomplished, North Carolina Republicans *celebrated* trimming black access to the voting booth.

Reportedly, an investigation by the Indianapolis Star found that policies by state and local Republicans in Indiana have restricted voting in predominantly Democratic areas — while expanding voting access in Republican-held areas. Simultaneously, in Indiana, once it became clear that black people could determine the outcome of an election, case-in-point when Barack Obama carried the state in 2008, the Republicans mobilized to suppress the Black vote by impeding their access to the polls. At the heart of the controversy: *early voting stations.*

The investigation, found that in Hamilton County, a Republican-majority area, officials had added two additional early voting stations, bringing the number of stations to one for every 100,000 residents.

Nevertheless, in Marion County — a county that votes more Democratic, has a large African-American population, and includes Indianapolis, the state's largest city. The Republican member of the election board blocked additional stations and prevented the continuation of satellite sites that existed during the 2008 election.

Reportedly, Election boards in Indiana have three people — a Democrat, a Republican, and the county clerk — and, since 2001, any decision to expand early voting requires a unanimous vote. The Republican member of the Marion county board has repeatedly blocked efforts to expand early voting since 2010.

In 2013, the Republican-controlled legislature passed a law, while Vice President Mike Pence was the governor - that specifically limited the processing of absentee ballots — which are used for early voting — to one site for counties with more than 325,000 people, without unanimous approval from the election board. Subsequently, in Marion, that meant one site for the more than 700,000 voters in the county.

Have the changes had an impact? As Indianapolis Star's Fatima Hussein writes:

The number of in-person absentee ballots cast in Hamilton County rose from 32,729 in 2008 to 53,608 in 2016, representing a 63 percent increase. At the same time, there was a 26 percent decrease in Marion County, from 93,316 to 68,599. During that period, the percentage of absentee ballots rose from 25 percent to 34 percent in Hamilton County and fell from 24 percent to 19 percent in Marion County.

This investigation came amid a lawsuit filed in May by Common Cause Indiana and the Indianapolis chapter of the NAACP against Republican officials. It alleges that the lack of voting stations in these areas constitutes discrimination.

Meanwhile, in 2017, Indiana passed a law allowing the state to purge voters from the rolls without notifying them, based on information from the controversial Crosscheck system. The Indiana NAACP and League of Women Voters have filed a federal lawsuit against Connie Lawson, Indiana's Secretary of State, to stop the purges. In June 2018, a federal judge ruled that the law violated the National Voter Registration Act.

FAST FORWARD: It seems like some states have all the luck. When Colorado's 3.5 million voters help select a president this fall, fortunately, their choice will be made almost entirely vote-by-mail. This will happen via ballots in postage-paid envelopes dropped off in mailboxes or, more commonly, in bins scattered statewide.

Alabama sees it differently for now. As the law currently stands, all voters must cast their ballots on Election Day, at their designated polling places unless they vote by absentee ballot. Plus, getting an absentee ballot is so hard that fewer than 55,000 of 1.7 million voters cast one in the last election.

Election experts, voting rights advocates, and a chorus of Democrats are urging states to switch as much as is possible to voting by mail for the November election. Their objective to ensure that the vote is not plagued by the same nightmare scenario that occurred this week in Wisconsin of voters in masks and gloves going to polls or staying home — amid the possible prolonged coronavirus pandemic.

The Republican governor of New Hampshire, Chris Sununu, endorsed the idea recently. Saying the state would hold its election by mail in November if health risks were still an issue. The Republican secretary of state in Iowa, Paul Pate, raised the same prospect this week. Elsewhere, Republican opposition, like court filings and President Trump's baseless charge that voting by mail is riddled with fraud, leaves the future of that effort in doubt. However, remaining optimistic - a change could emerge.

According to, Judd Choate, the state elections director in Colorado, which made the change six years ago: "Switching to voting by mail, even in states with no history of it, can be done, and quite likely it may need to be done… It is just a matter of how bumpy it is."

Those potential bumps got vividly illustrated by a sample timeline prepared for states by the federal Election Assistance Commission. This lays out scores of steps, like procuring software, training staff, and getting federal post office approval of ballot envelopes, that would have to get completed before Election Day in November.

In states where voters' ballots are fed by hand into scanners at every precinct would now have to buy high-speed scanners to tabulate votes to facilitate. Then probably move most counting to a central location to save money. People would have to get hired and trained to process ballots and verify a vast number of signatures. And additional workers would have to deal with large amounts of voters whose ballots were rejected because their signatures had changed or their marks for a candidate were unclear. This extends a call for more volunteers in this upcoming presidential election.

Voters would have to acclimate to navigating a balloting process most had never experienced. According to David J. Becker, the director of the Center for Election Innovation and Research, a nonprofit organization working to promote public confidence in elections by making them better run:

"A presidential election sees the largest percentage of infrequent voters …They are not familiar with how to mark a ballot or what the deadline is, and that is particularly true when you have a complicated ballot. Florida probably will see a 10-page ballot."

David continued:

"Voting by mail is voting without a safety net … If you are in a polling place and make two marks on a ballot for president, the machine will reject the ballot."

I'm hopeful some entity would release a video to help voters-by-mail for the first time - make a smooth, accurate transition.

17

It is a covert political tactic: At least every 10 years, states, redraw district lines based on population data gathered in the US census. Legislators then use these district lines to allocate representation in Congress as well as state legislatures. When redistricting gets conducted accurately, district lines get redrawn to reflect population changes and racial diversity. Even so, to exploit voter suppression strategies, states use redistricting as a political apparatus to manipulate the outcome of elections.

Gerrymandering is this tactic of voter suppression. It is defined as a practice intended to establish an unfair political advantage for a particular party or group by manipulating district boundaries, most commonly used in first-past-the-post electoral systems.

Get familiar with these two terms when it comes to this tactic: Cracking and Packing. These two superior tactics get used in gerrymandering: "cracking" (i.e. diluting the voting power of the opposing party's supporters across many districts) and "packing" - concentrating the opposing Party's voting power in one community to reduce their voting power in other regions.

A third tactic, also of concern, is the homogenization of all districts - substantially a form of cracking where the majority party uses its superior numbers to guarantee the minority party never attains a majority in any region.

In addition to its use achieving desired electoral results for a particular party. Gerrymandering may be used to help or hinder a specific demographic, such as a political, ethnic, racial, linguistic, religious, or class group, such as in Northern Ireland, where boundaries were constructed to guarantee Protestant Unionist majorities.

The U.S. federal voting district boundaries that produce a majority of constituents representative of African-American or other racial minorities are known as "majority-minority districts". Gerrymandering can also get used to protecting incumbents. Wayne Dawkings describes it as politicians picking their voters instead of voters choosing their politicians.

The term *gerrymandering* is named after Elbridge Gerry - pronounced like "Gary", who, as Governor of Massachusetts in 1812, signed a bill that created a partisan district in the Boston area that was compared to the shape of a mythological salamander. The term has negative connotations, and gerrymandering is almost always considered a corruption of the democratic process. The resulting district is known as a *gerrymander*. The word is also a verb for the procedure.

The word gerrymander - originally written Gerry-mander, was used for the first time in the Boston Gazette - not to be confused with the original *Boston Gazette*, on 26 March 1812.

The word was created in reaction to a redrawing of Massachusetts state senate election districts under Governor Elbridge Gerry. In 1812, Gerry signed a bill that redistricted Massachusetts to benefit his Democratic-Republican Party. When mapped, one of the contorted districts in the Boston area was said to resemble the shape of a mythological salamander.[7]

Gerrymander is a portmanteau of the governor's last name and the word *salamander*.

The redistricting was a notable success for Gerry's Democratic-Republican Party. Although in the 1812 election, both the Massachusetts House and governorship were won by Federalists by a comfortable margin and cost Gerry his job, the redistricted state Senate remained firmly in Democratic-Republican hands.

Gerrymandering once again as presented itself centerstage in 2020. The Trump administration is heating its heels to embark on the 2020 census. Having his way will determine our politics for years to come.

Meanwhile, the administration attempted adding a citizenship question to the upcoming census. The Commerce Department's decision to ask Census respondents about their citizenship status, for the first time since 1950, looked like a deliberate attempt to drill down on voter suppression.

Last year, the ACLU sued the Trump administration regarding that potential inclusion. It was successfully blocked. Reportedly, document attacking immigrants was discovered. Proving it was the Commerce Secretary Wilbur Ross lied to Congress to conceal it.

Without Census data on citizens and noncitizens, red states would have no means of giving voters-only districting a try.

18

Enforced until 1965, and widely debated among blacks, Jim Crow laws were state and local laws that enforced racial segregation in the Southern United States. All were enacted in the late 19th and early 20th centuries by white Democratic-dominated state legislatures after the Reconstruction period.

The source of the phrase "Jim Crow" has often been attributed to "Jump Jim Crow". A song-and-dance caricature of blacks performed by white actor Thomas D. Rice in blackface, which first surfaced in 1832 and was used to satirize Andrew Jackson's populist policies.

As a result of Rice's fame, "Jim Crow" by 1838 had become a pejorative expression meaning *Negro*. When southern legislatures passed laws of racial segregation directed against blacks at the end of the 19th century, these statutes became known as Jim Crow laws.

During this Reconstruction period of 1865–1877, federal laws provided civil rights protections in the U.S. South for freedmen, the African Americans who had formerly been slaves, and the minority of blacks who had been free before the war. In the 1870s, Democrats gradually regained power in the Southern legislatures.

Thereby, having used insurgent paramilitary groups, such as the White League and the Red Shirts, to disrupt Republican organizing, run Republican officeholders out of town, and intimidate blacks to suppress their voting.

Meanwhile, in 1877, a national Democratic Party compromise to gain Southern support in the presidential election - a corrupt bargain, resulted in the Government's withdrawing the last of the federal troops from the South. White Democrats had regained political power in every Southern state.

Coincidentally, Black got elected to local offices throughout the 1880s, but their voting got suppressed for state and national elections. Democrats passed laws to make voter registration and electoral rules more restrictive, with the result that political participation by most blacks and many poor whites began to decrease.

Between 1890 and 1910, ten of the eleven former Confederate states, starting with Mississippi, passed new constitutions or amendments that effectively disenfranchised most blacks and tens of thousands of poor whites through a combination of poll taxes, literacy and comprehension tests, and residency and record-keeping requirements.

In the meantime, voter turnout dropped drastically through the South as a result of such measures. In Louisiana, by 1900, black voters were reduced to 5,320 on the rolls, although they comprised the majority of the state's population.

By 1910, only 730 blacks got registered, less than 0.5% of eligible black men.

In 27 of the state's 60 parishes, not a single black voter was registered any longer; in 9 more parishes, only one black voter was.

The cumulative effect in North Carolina meant that black voters were eliminated from voter rolls during the period from 1896–1904. The growth of their thriving middle class was slowed. In North Carolina and other Southern states, blacks suffered from being made invisible in the political system:

Within a decade of disfranchisement, the white supremacy campaign had erased the image of the black middle class from the minds of white North Carolinians.

In Alabama, tens of thousands of poor whites got disenfranchised, although initially, legislators had promised them they would not be affected adversely by the new restrictions.

In some cases, progressive measures intended to reduce election fraud, such as the Eight Box Law in South Carolina, acted against black and white voters. They were illiterate, as they could not follow the directions.

Meanwhile, the separation of African Americans from the general white population was becoming legalized and formalized during the Progressive Era - 1890s–1920s, it was also becoming customary. For instance, even in cases in which Jim Crow laws did not expressly forbid black people from participating in sports or recreation, a segregated culture had become common.

Those laws, though now as water under the bridge, still irritates - as swallowing a fishbone when it comes to Blacks.

19

Reportedly, in the 2002 New Hampshire Senate election a phone jamming scandal emerged. Republican officials attempted to reduce the number of Democratic voters by paying professional telemarketers in Idaho to make repeated hang-up calls to the telephone numbers used by the Democratic Party's ride-to-the-polls phone lines on election day. In this ploy of tying up the lines, voters seeking rides from the Democratic Party would have more difficulty reaching the party to ask for transportation to and from their polling places.

It is a given that a vast percentage of Blacks do not drive.

Meanwhile, during the 2004 presidential election, allegations surfaced in several states that a private group, Voters Outreach of America, which had been empowered by the individual states, had collected and submitted Republican voter registration forms. While inappropriately discarding voter registration forms where the new voter had chosen to register with the Democratic Party.

Such people would believe they had registered to vote and would only discover on election day that they were not registered and could not cast a ballot.

Michigan Republican state legislator John Pappageorge was quoted as saying:

"If we do not suppress the Detroit vote, we're going to have a tough time in this election."

Reportedly, in 2006, four employees of candidate John Kerry's campaign were convicted of slashing the tires of 25 vans rented by the Wisconsin state Republican Party which were to be used for driving Republican voters and monitors to the polls. They received jail terms of four to six months. At the campaign workers' sentencing, Judge Michael B. Brennan told the defendants:

"Voter suppression has no place in our Country. Your crime took away that right to vote for some citizens." Meanwhile, in 2006, during the Virginia U.S. Senate election, Secretary of the Virginia State Board of Elections Jean Jensen concluded that incidents of voter suppression appeared widespread and deliberate. Documented events of voter suppression include:

- Democratic voters receiving calls incorrectly informing them voting will lead to arrest.
- Widespread calls fraudulently claiming to be "[Democratic Senate candidate Jim] Webb Volunteers," falsely telling voters their voting location had changed.
- Fliers paid for by the Republican Party, stating "SKIP THIS ELECTION" that allegedly attempted to suppress African-American turnout.

The FBI, has since launched an investigation into the suppression attempts. Despite the allegations, Democrat Jim Webb narrowly defeated incumbent George Allen.

Relatedly, on September 16, 2008, attorneys for then-Democratic presidential candidate Barack Obama announced their intention to seek an injunction to stop an alleged caging scheme in Michigan. It got alleged that the Michigan Republican Party used home foreclosure lists to challenge voters who used their foreclosed homes as their primary addresses at the polls. Michigan GOP officials called the suit "desperate". A federal appeals court ordered the reinstatement of 5,500 voters wrongly purged from the voter rolls by the state.

The conservative nonprofit Minnesota Majority reportedly made phone calls claiming that the Minnesota Secretary of State had concerns about the validity of voters' registration. Their actions were referred to the Ramsey County attorney's office.

20

I have touched on the subject of long lines at polls earlier and how it poses a hazard for Black voters – equating to voter suppression. For years, on the Sunday before each election, black churches in Cleveland, Ohio, would load their congregations onto buses and head to the polls to vote. This was so evident in recent elections and footage many blacks carpooling in vans - shown on Cable News.

Even though Ohio's population is 28 percent black, 56 percent of Cuyahoga County's weekend voters in the 2008 election were black.

Early Voting, proved strategic in Obama's 2008 election. It helped elect the first black president. Ohio saw the problem and decided to find a solution. They made sure that would never happen again.

Voting early and extended voting hours are critical to black voters because African Americans are twice as likely to work jobs that pay hourly wages — waiting in line to vote costs black voters both time and money. Yet, Ohio and Nebraska have now reduced the days and hours citizens are allowed to vote.

If there are two neighborhoods in the same city, one with mostly white voters and one with primarily black and Hispanic voters, those in the white communities will have a shorter wait time at the polls. As I mentioned, earlier Blacks need to get involved by volunteering at polling stations in their state.

Reportedly, in the 2016 Elections, black people waited an average of 16 minutes to vote, while white voters waited less than 10 minutes, according to a Massachusetts Institute of Technology voter survey. It got drawn to my attention that Georgia is currently trying to force Atlanta to close its polls an hour early on election day. Georgia has a record of Black voter suppression – displayed in the 2018 mid-terms and previous elections, so that move got baked in.

Meanwhile, in North Carolina, during the 2016 election, black early voting was down 8.7 percent. A North Carolina federal court found that cuts to the state's early voting hours were part of a Republican strategy to decrease black turnout in the US.
Meanwhile, Michigan will have an initiative on its November ballot to extend early voting hours. A study also showed that voting lines are shortest at noon, at 5 p.m., and then at the end of the day.

Some states offer the convenience of early voting. If you reside in such a state, please take advantage of its early voting and bring out the vote!

21

An aging Republican Party made up mostly of white men carrying the DNA of the civil rights era. Collaboratively, they have endeavored to prey on Blacks.

The hate crimes of the 60s, such as lynching, police brutality, the burning of churches, violence against health care providers, and the transport of persons - particularly women and children for enslavement or forced labor are a collection of hate crimes inflicted on blacks back then.

In addition to police brutality, voter suppression has been the main carry-over. Shortly after losing its second presidential election to Barack Obama, the Republican party looked themselves in the mirror. The image wasn't a magnificent sight. In the backdrop, they no doubt saw the hate crimes of the sixties.

In 2013, the Republican National Committee declared that the Republican Party must be committed to building a lasting relationship within the African American community annually, centered around a spirit of caring. Months later, those same Republicans cheered a Supreme court decision that maimed the Voting Rights Act. Not too long thereafter, Birtherism was created.

With Trump in the White House, splinters from the Civil Rights era reappeared. A Unite the Right rally, which was a white supremacist rally, occurred in Charlottesville, Virginia, from August 11 to 12, 2017. Jason Kessler, the organizer of the rally, had been protesting for months the proposed removal of a statue of Robert E. Lee in Emancipation Park in Charlottesville.

Meanwhile, on those dates, individuals, and groups of different beliefs and tactics demonstrated against the rally. Many counter-protesters were ready to turn out despite the threat of violence. Hundreds of torch-bearing white nationalists marched through the University of Virginia campus, chanting slogans such as "blood and soil" and "Jews will not replace us."

On the second day, more violence erupted as white nationalists and protesters clashed in downtown Charlottesville. One woman, Heather Heyer, was killed, and dozens more were injured when a white nationalist backed his car into a crowd of protesters.

James Fields Jr., the suspected driver, was arrested and has already been charged with federal hate crimes in Heyer's death, as well as state murder charges. Additionally, four people have gotten charged with violating anti-riot laws in connection with the deadly event.

All four men, who live in California, are part of the "Rise Above Movement," a white supremacist group, prosecutors said.

United States Attorney Thomas Cullen said later at a press conference.

"I think we will have several witnesses, in addition to video and other evidence, that establishes how these four individuals incited a riot, committed acts of violence and therefore violated federal law,"

Of the incident, President Trump at a press conference weighed in:

"You also had people that were very fine people, on both sides."

Months later, he recanted: *As I said on -- remember this -- Saturday, we condemn in the strongest possible terms this egregious display of hatred, bigotry and violence. It has no place in America. And when I went on from there. Now, here's the thing. As to -- excuse me -- excuse me -- take it nice and easy. Here's the thing. When I make a statement, I like to be correct. I want the facts. This event just happened. In fact, a lot of the event didn't even happen yet, as we were speaking. This event just happened. Before I make a statement, I need the facts. So, I don't want to rush into a statement. So making the statement when I made it was excellent. In fact, the young woman who I hear is a fantastic young woman, and it was on NBC, her mother wrote me and said through, I guess, Twitter, social media, the nicest things and I very much appreciate that. I hear she was a fine, a really -- actually, an incredible young woman. But her mother on Twitter thanked me for what I said. And honestly, if the press were not fake and if it was honest, the press would have said what I said was very nice. But unlike you and unlike -- excuse me -- unlike you and unlike the media, before I make a statement, I like to know the facts.*

The roots of the civil rights era run deep!

Racism which has never left. It is once again seeding in the United States. The terror of family separation and babies placed in cages at the southern border is yet another example of "Making America Hate Again".

22

It is a well-known fact that a higher percentage of Black men wind up in prison more than any other race in the United States. While some are guilty of the crimes omitted, a majority of them are not. They just happen to be black. This strategy is yet another ploy used to suppress the Black vote.

In June 1964, these three young men: Andrew Goodman, James Chaney, and Michael Schwerner were working in Mississippi to help African

Americans obtain their civil rights in voting, education, and employment.

On June 21, 1964, they visited a church that had been fire-bombed near Philadelphia, Mississippi. After leaving the crime scene, the young men were arrested by members of the Neshoba County Sheriff's Department for speeding. Later that night, the trio disappeared.

Within a few days of the disappearance, the FBI began an investigation, and members of the U.S. Department of Justice's Civil Rights Division visited Mississippi as their investigation escalated. Two months later, on August 4, 1964, a paid informant of the FBI, revealed the location of the bodies of the three young civil rights workers. Bullet wounds not only showed their cause of death, but they had been severely beaten.

Subsequently, in December 1964, 19 white men, including the sheriff and his deputy, were arrested on state conspiracy charges, but the charges got dropped. In 1967, after a federal prosecution for conspiracy to deny the young men's civil rights, seven white men were convicted.

Meanwhile, a hate crime case rocked the nation in March 1991. In Los Angeles, California, the beating of Rodney king illuminated the spotlight. After police officers who allegedly beat King got acquitted in that state trial, explosive riots broke out in Central LA.

The Justice Department's Civil Rights Division and US Attorney then prosecuted the officers under a federal criminal, civil rights statute.

Knowing your rights is very important in this country. It's comforting knowing that the U.S. Department of Justice's Civil Rights Division also enforces federal criminal, civil rights laws that involve "hate crimes." Crimes committed against individuals or institutions because of their race, ethnic background, or religion remains intolerable in the US.

Back in 1996, a string of church arsons, especially in a large number of African-American churches, led President Bill Clinton to form a special task force, known as the National Church Arson Task Force.

This legal arm was made up of lawyers from the Civil Rights Division, agents of the Bureau of Alcohol, Tobacco and Firearms, and agents of the Federal Bureau of Investigation. This Task Force was assigned to investigate and prosecute these arsonists under the federal criminal, civil rights statutes.

Whether you have witnessed a hate crime or are the victim of such an offense, you should know that state and federal laws can help you get the justice you deserve. While there may be civil remedies for certain discriminatory acts, hate crimes are taken much more seriously and should be investigated promptly. Consider speaking with a local civil rights attorney to learn more.

23

Black voters are the base of the Democratic Party and held significant sway in the primary elections.

Reportedly, Black voters make up about 20% of all Democratic voters, according to 2016 primary exit polls and 2018 data from the Pew Research Center.

Relatedly, about the same percentage of Democrats identified themselves as *very liberal* in the average 2016 primary with an exit poll as the percentage of Democrats who said they were black. The following gives an overview of the historic Black Vote in Primary Elections, compared to general election projections.

- Unlike college-educated whites and very liberal Democrats, black voters have consistently been a large portion of the Democratic base.

- Based on the stats in the 1980 election, black voters made up about 20% of Democrat Jimmy Carter's vote. In 2000, they were about 20% of Democrat Al Gore's base of support against George W. Bush.

- Black voters have voted very similarly to one another in recent competitive contests. Hillary Clinton won about 80% of the black vote in the 2016 primary.

- Barack Obama won about 80% of it in the 2008 primary. Although neither the 2004 or 2000 primary season went on for any extended length to fully grasp how all black Democrats felt, John Kerry and Al Gore both dominated the black vote in early contests and did better than they did with white voters.

- Bill Clinton won about 70% of the black vote in 1992. Jesse Jackson won over 75% of the black vote in both his 1984 and 1988 bids.

- The vast majority of Democrats in South Carolina are black, and Clinton used this to her advantage when she lost New Hampshire and barely beat Sanders in Iowa and Nevada.

- Even if the eventual Democratic nominee does not win the black vote, they will still need black voters to vote massively for them in the general election.

- Black voters are a vital part of the Democratic Party in the primary and general elections. Democratic candidates are wise to reach out to them on many platforms and in many forums.

Just slightly more Democrats are whites with a college degree than are black. Relatedly, black voters make up about the same slice of the Democratic Party.

24

Jim Clyburn is Representative of South Carolina, also House Majority Whip. Clyburn is classified as a King-Maker. Joe Biden, the past Vice President who shouldered President Barack Obama between 2008 and 2016.

Biden entered the 2020 race as a presidential candidate on a high with much support. Only to have his campaign dwarfed by the Ukraine scandal, which placed his son Hunter Biden center stage. The scandal, orchestrated by President Trump and his personal lawyer Rudy Giuliani. A tactic set to bring down Joe Biden. As a result of this ploy, President Trump was impeached, and it almost cost him the presidency had he not been acquitted mainly due to the support of a Republican-led senate.

Hunter Biden had previously worked for a Ukrainian company, Burisma. It was alleged the said company was a corruption nest at the time of Hunter's involvement as he sat on their board.

Subsequently, Joe Biden fell way behind in the polls while contrastingly, he led the in polls before the Ukraine scandal broke. As the primary voting began, he lost the Iowa caucus, the New Hampshire Primary, and then the Nevada caucus. With the South Carolina Primary in view.

It was then that Jim Clyburn gave him that all-important endorsement three days ahead of the primary, which placed Joe Biden center stage.

Biden, then won that South Carolina primary by a landslide – a state where the Black Vote matter. He followed it up by sweeping the southern states versus his opponent Bernie sanders.

Subsequently, Joe Biden became the presidential nominee. Later, he received the endorsement of his competitor Bernie Sanders, Elizabeth Warren and many others including former President Barack Obama.

25

Senator and 2020 Presidential Candidate Kamila Harris recently unveiled the Vote Safe Act, expecting a bi-partisan vote in its passage. According to Harris, the bill will be three-pronged.

1. Expand Vote-By-Mail.
2. Facilitate early voting, proposing at least 20 days early voting.

3. It expands access and safety. That states consider curbside voting.

More access for indigenous people – native American population, e.g., Alaskan population, expand access to voters with disabilities. To have the federal government encouraging states to make voting in this climate safe and accessible to all voters.

When asked about bi-partisan support, Senator Harris said: "I hope there is bipartisan support. I think there will be. Right now, we are seeking bipartisan support. When you look at Wisconsin, the recent election and that they had to close over 100 polling places because they did not have the workers because they did not have the infrastructure to accommodate voting in this era of the pandemic."

She said.

"So, it is the smart thing to do, and it should be bi-partisan...and we need to make sure everyone has access and they can vote in a safe way."

Senator Harris further elaborated.

About The Author

John A. Andrews, screenwriter, producer, playwright, director, and author of several books. As an author of almost 50 books in the genre on relationships, personal development, faith-based, and vivid engaging novels. Also, a playwright and screenwriter.

John is sought after as a motivational speaker to address success principles to young adults. He makes an impact in the lives of others because of his passion and commitment to make a difference in his life and the world.

Being a father of three sons propels John even more in his desire to see teens succeed. Andrews, a divorced dad of three sons Jonathan 24, Jefferri 22, and Jamison 19. Andrews was born in the Islands of St. Vincent and the Grenadines. His two eldest sons are also writers and wrote their first two novels while teenagers.

Andrews grew up in a home of five sisters and three brothers. He recounts: "My parents were all about values: work hard, love God, and never give up on your dreams." Self-educated, John developed an interest in music. Although lacking formal education, he later put his knowledge and passion to good use, moonlighting as a disc jockey in New York. This paved the way for further exploration in the world of entertainment. In 1994 John caught the acting bug. Leaving the Big Apple for Hollywood over a decade ago not only put several national TV commercials under his belt but helped him to find his niche. He also appeared in the movie John Q starring Denzel Washington.

His passion for writing started in 2002 when he was denied the rights to a 1970's classic film, which he so badly wanted to remake. In 2007, while etching two of his original screenplays, he published his first book "The 5 Steps to Changing Your Life"

In 2008 he not only published his second book but also wrote 7 additional books that year, and produced the docu-drama based on his second book; *Spread Some Love (Relationships 101).*

Currently, he just published book 47 and working on 48, 49 and 50. With several in the movie and TV pipeline.

See Imdb: http://www.imdb.com/title/tt0854677/.

Visit: **A L I**

www.JohnAAndrews.com

THE BOTCHED AMENDMENT

LADERA HEIGHTS
LA
UNDERCOVER
JOHN A. ANDREWS

AGENT
O'GARRO
II
WHERE IS THE BODY?
A THRILLER
COMING
SOON
FROM THE CREATOR OF
RUDE BUAY
RENEGADE COPS
&
WHODUNIT CHRONICLES
JOHN A.
ANDREWS
#1 INTERNATIONAL BESTSELLING AUTHOR

THE
INSIDE
JOB
RENEGADE COPS 2
JOHN A. ANDREWS
CREATOR OF
THE RUDE BUAY SERIES
&
THE WHODUNIT CHRONICLES

JOHN A. ANDREWS
gzhou
Lufeng
#1 INTERNATIONAL BESTSELLING AUTHOR
Hong Kong
The Untitled
HONG KONG
Novel

DESIREE O'GARRO

THE LETHAL KID

A TEEN THRILLER
FROM THE CREATORS OF
RUDE BUAY
AGENT O'GARRO
RENEGADE COPS
A SNITCH ON TIME
WHO SHOT THE SHERIFF?
&
THE MACOS ADVENTURE

#1 INTERNATIONAL BESTSELLING AUTHOR

JOHN A. ANDREWS

&

*JEFFERRI ANDREWS

A TEEN FRIENDLY NOVEL

NEW
RELEASES

A JOHN ANDREWS FILM
Born to Write
A TRUE
HOLLYWOOD STORY

THE UNITED STATES PANDEMIC
FIGHTING THE INVISIBLE ENEMY
FROM THE AUTHOR OF PANDEMIC WARFARE
JOHN A. ANDREWS
"A MEDICAL THRILLER"
THE AFTERMATH OF
COVID - 19

JOHN A. ANDREWS
FIGHTING AGAINST THE INVISIBLE ENEMY
PANDEMIC WARFARE
It began in Wuhan, China. Now crippling the world with an increasing death toll in its grasp...
THE MYSTERY BEHIND COVID - 19
#1 INTERNATIONAL BESTSELLER

FROM THE CREATOR OF *WHO SHOT THE SHERIFF?*

JOHN A. ANDREWS

UNTIL DEATH DO US PART

A NOVEL

ONE FOOT IN *NEW YORK UNDERCOVER*
THE OTHER IN *ALFRED HITCHCOCK PRESENTS*

124
N.Y.C ©
NEW YORK CONNIVERS
FROM THE CREATOR OF WHO SHOT THE SHERIFF?
JOHN A. ANDREWS
CATCH HER BEFORE SHE STRIKES AGAIN
LOUISE DIPSON
THE PREDATOR
"THIS ISN'T JUST A NOVEL
IT'S A HANDFUL"
ONE FOOT IN NEW YORK UNDERCOVER
THE OTHER IN ALFRED HITCHCOCK PRESENTS

NYC
NEW YORK CONNIVERS
FROM THE CREATOR OF WHO SHOT THE SHERIFF?

JOHN A. ANDREWS
NEW YORK CITY BLUES
THE UNDERGROUND OPERATION
A NOVEL
ONE FOOT IN NEW YORK UNDERCOVER
THE OTHER IN ALFRED HITCHCOCK PRESENTS

Climbing Up From The Bottom AUTHOR
JOHN A. ANDREWS
Dare To Make A Difference (Success 101)
Spread Some Love (Relationships 101)
The 5 Steps To Changing Your Life
THE SUCCESS TRIANGLE™
Three Books In One Volume
Including DARE TO MAKE A DIFFERENCE

I'M STILL STANDING
WHEN THE DUST SETTLES
starring
John A. Andrews
BIOGRAPHY REVISED

A COLLECTOR'S ITEM
UNSTOPPABLE
JOHN A. ANDREWS
ACTION-THRILLER Series
RUDE BUAY
VOLUMES 1-3

AGENT
O'GARRO
TIME IS THE ENEMY
A THRILLER
COMING SOON
FROM THE CREATOR OF
RUDE BUAY
RENEGADE COPS
DESIREE O'GARRO
&
WHO SHOT THE SHERIFF?
A TEEN-FRIENDLY NOVEL
JOHN A. ANDREWS
#1 INTERNATIONAL BESTSELLER

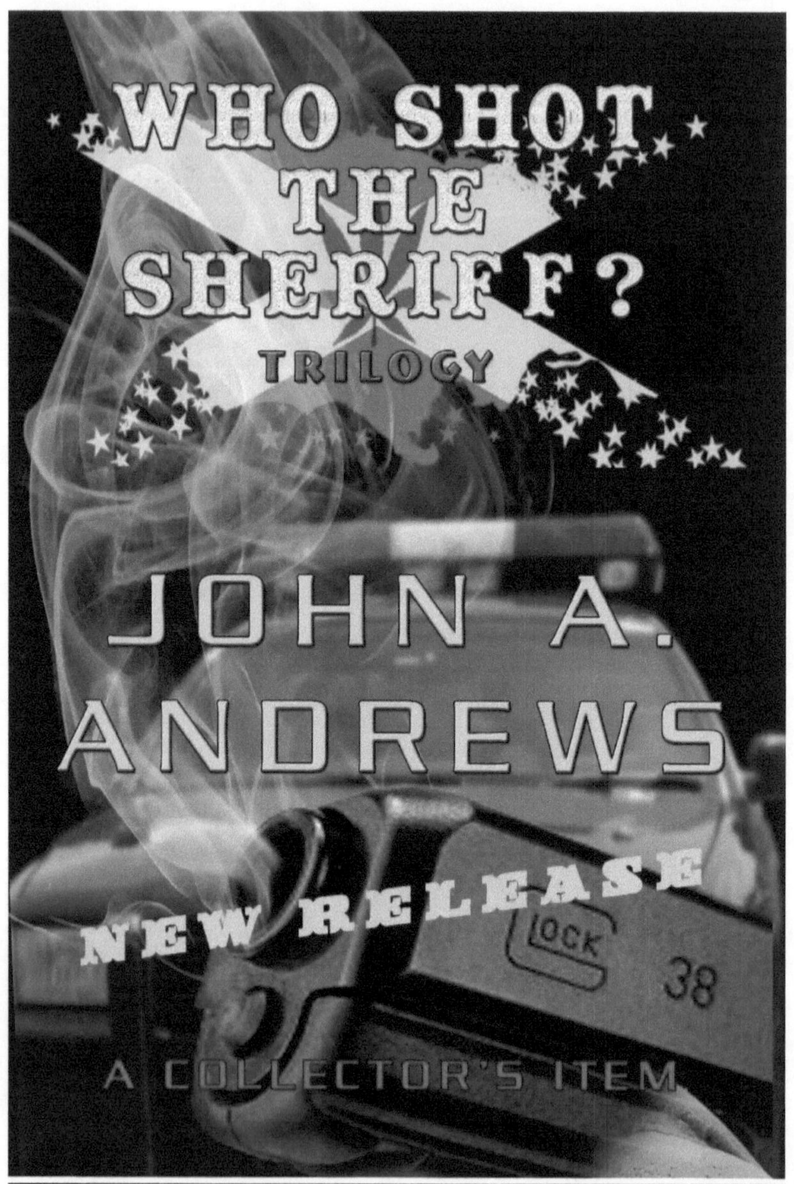
WHO SHOT THE SHERIFF?
TRILOGY
JOHN A. ANDREWS
NEW RELEASE
GLOCK 38
A COLLECTOR'S ITEM

A JOHN ANDREWS FILM
THE JURY
BASED ON
WHO SHOT THE
SHERIFF?
GLOCK 38
WRITTEN BY: JOHN A. ANDREWS PRODUCED BY: PATRICK MCINTIRE,
MICHAEL W. REID, JOHN ANDREWS
EXECUTIVE PRODUCERS: SELENA SMITH & JANIS PHILLIP
DIRECTED BY: JOHN ANDREWS.
AN A L I PICTURES PRODUCTION

OTHER RELEASES

How I Wrote 8 Books In One Year
JOHN A. ANDREWS
8
A
Author of
TOTAL COMMITTMENT
The Mindset Of Champions

ANDREWS
"QUOTES"
Unlimited
John A. Andrews
National Bestselling Author
of
Rude Buay ... The Unstoppable

ANDREWS
"QUOTES"
UNLIMITED
Vol. II
Over 400 Quotes From Over 18 Books!
John A. Andrews
National Bestselling Author of
RUDE BUAY ... THE UNSTOPPABLE

DARE TO MAKE A DIFFERENCE
SUCCESS 101
FOR TEENS
JOHN A. ANDREWS
#1 INTERNATIONAL BESTSELLING AUTHOR

ANDREWS
The FIVE
"Ps"
FOR TEENS
National Bestselling Author
John A. Andrews

DARE TO MAKE A DIFFERENCE
SUCCESS 101
FOR
ADULTS
#1 INTERNATIONAL BESTSELLING AUTHOR
JOHN A. ANDREWS

National Bestselling Author of
Rude Buay ... The Unstoppable

THE 5
STEPS TO
CHANGING
YOUR LIFE
BY: JOHN A. ANDREWS

JOHN A. ANDREWS

THE MUSICAL©

**FROM THE CREATOR OF
RUDE BUAY
THE WHODUNIT CHRONICLES
&
THE CHURCH ON FIRE**

SO MANY ARE TRYING TO GO TO HEAVEN
WITHOUT FIRST BUILDING A HEAVEN
HERE ON EARTH...
#1 INTERNATIONAL BESTSELLER

JOHN A. ANDREWS
CREATOR OF:
THE CHURCH ... A HOSPITAAL?
&
THE CHURCH ON FIRE

COMING ON SUNDAYS
2019 TBA
THAT CONNECTS
PRAISE
HEAVEN & EARTH
THE
CHURCH
ON FIRE
THE MUSICAL®
WRITTEN & DIRECTED BY JOHN A. ANDREWS

By National Bestselling Author of Rude Buay ... The Unstoppable
TOTAL COMMITMENT
The Mindset of Champions
JOHN A. ANDREWS

NATIONAL BESTSELLING AUTHOR
John A. Andrews
spread
some
LOVE
Relationships 101
REVISED EDITION

A SNITCH
ON TIME
DA POLICE
It's Nothing New For a Black Man
Without a Gun To be Killed…
Writer & Director
JOHN A. ANDREWS

AUTHOR OF NATIONAL BESTSELLER RUDE BUAY ... THE UNSTOPPABLE
Whose Woman
Was She?
A TRUE
HOLLYWOOD
STORY...
John A. Andrews

THE UNSTOPPABLE
JOHN A. ANDREWS
AN INTERNATIONAL
SECRET SERVICE AGENT
NOVEL SERIES...
An A L I Pictures 2016 Production
COMING TO THE BIG SCREEN
&
VIDEO GAME
"THINK GTA4 PLUS"
RUDE BUAY
#1 International Bestseller

#1 International Bestselling Author
JOHN A. ANDREWS
THE UNTOUCHABLE
RUDE BUAY
An International
Secret Service Agent
Novel Series...
2

#1 INTERNATIONAL BESTSELLING AUTHOR
SHATTERPROOF
RUDE BUAY ®3
JOHN A. ANDREWS

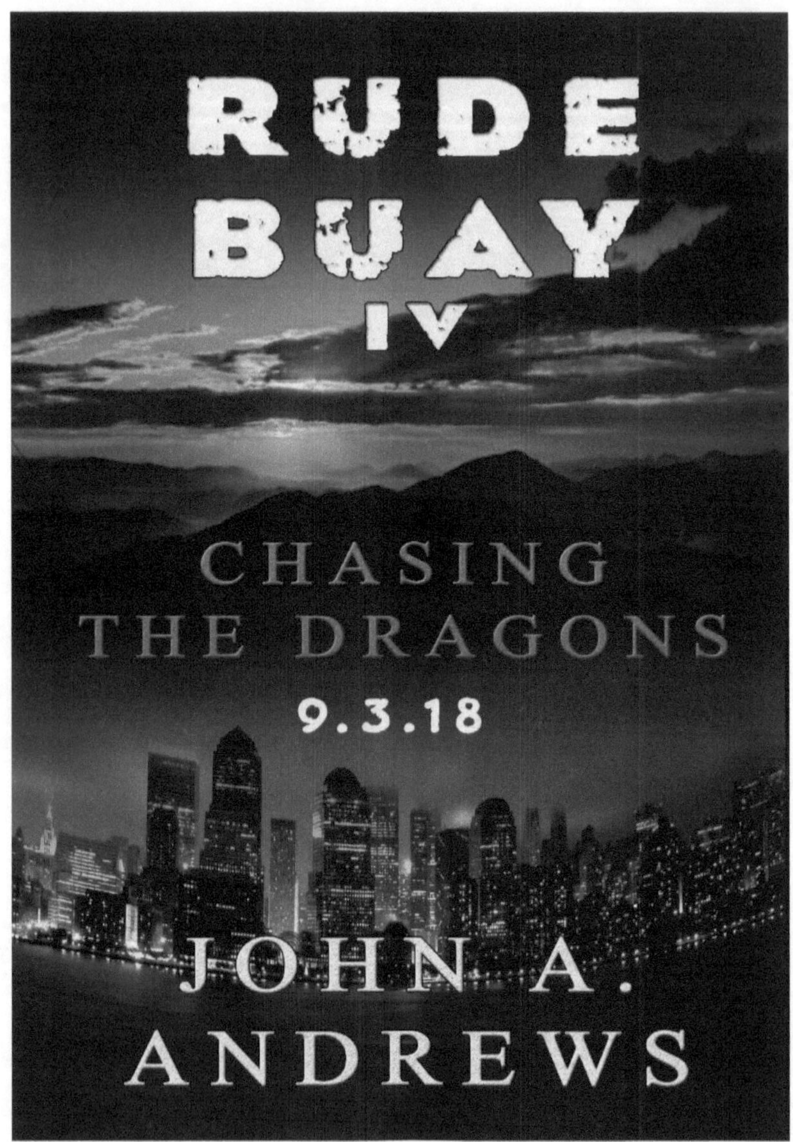
RUDE
BUAY
IV
CHASING
THE DRAGONS
9.3.18
JOHN A.
ANDREWS

国作家
硬迪·布瑞
THE UNSTOPPABLE
永不言弃
JOHN A. ANDREWS

THE UNSTOPPABLE
NACIONAL SUPERVENTAS
CHICO RUDO
EL
IMPARABLE
JOHN A. ANDREWS

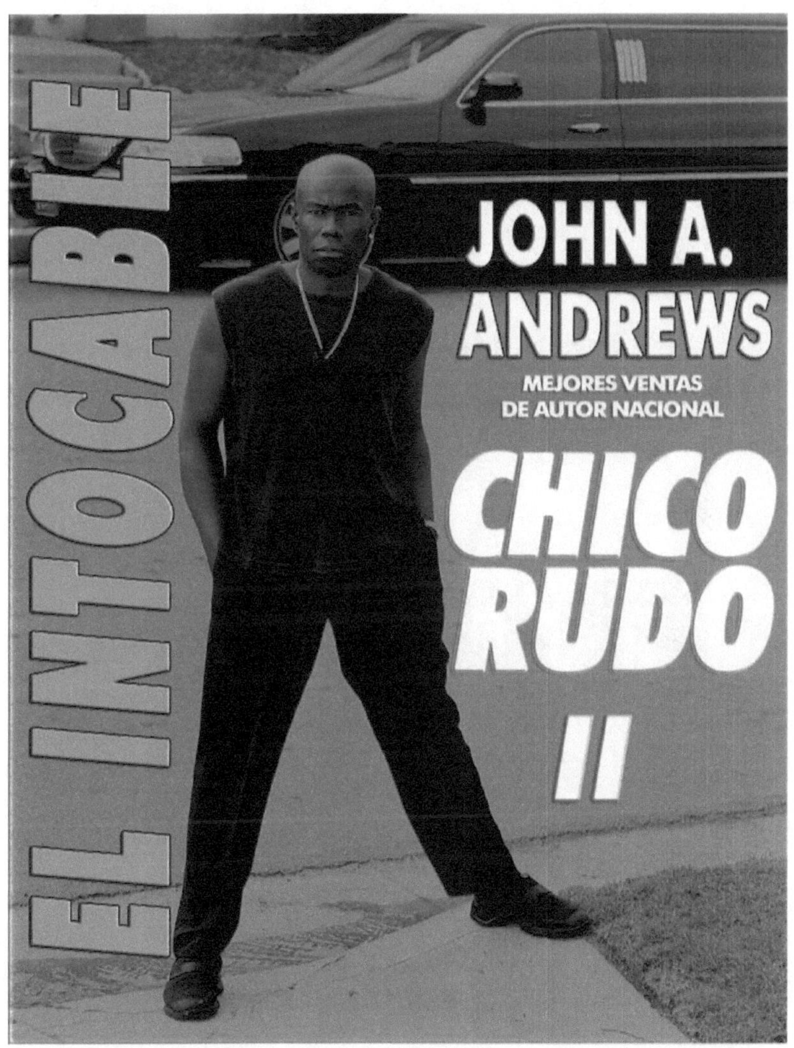

EL INTOCABLE
JOHN A. ANDREWS
MEJORES VENTAS DE AUTOR NACIONAL
CHICO RUDO II

CROSS
ATLANTIC
FIASCO
BLOOD IS THICKER THAN WATER
JOHN A. ANDREWS
Creator of
The RUDE BUAY Series
~ A Novel ~

WHO SHOT
THE SHERIFF?
The Hustle, The Flow, The Verdict.
COMING SOON.
GLOCK
38
A 2015 A L I Pictures Production
ALL
PICTURES

WHO SHOT
THE SHERIFF?
II
Let THE GAMES Begin.....
April 1, 2016
The MILTON ROGERS' CONSPIRACY
ALI
PICTURES
A 2016 A L I Pictures Production
GLOCK
38
JOHN A. ANDREWS
Co-written with Teen Authors
JONATHAN & JEFFERRI
ANDREWS

THE AUTHORITY SQUAD
THE
MACOS
ADVENTURE
2
A TEEN NOVEL
JONATHAN
&
JEFFERRI ANDREWS
With
International Bestselling Author
JOHN A. ANDREWS

BOOKS
THAT WILL
ENHANCE
YOUR
LIFE

AI
TM
PICTURES

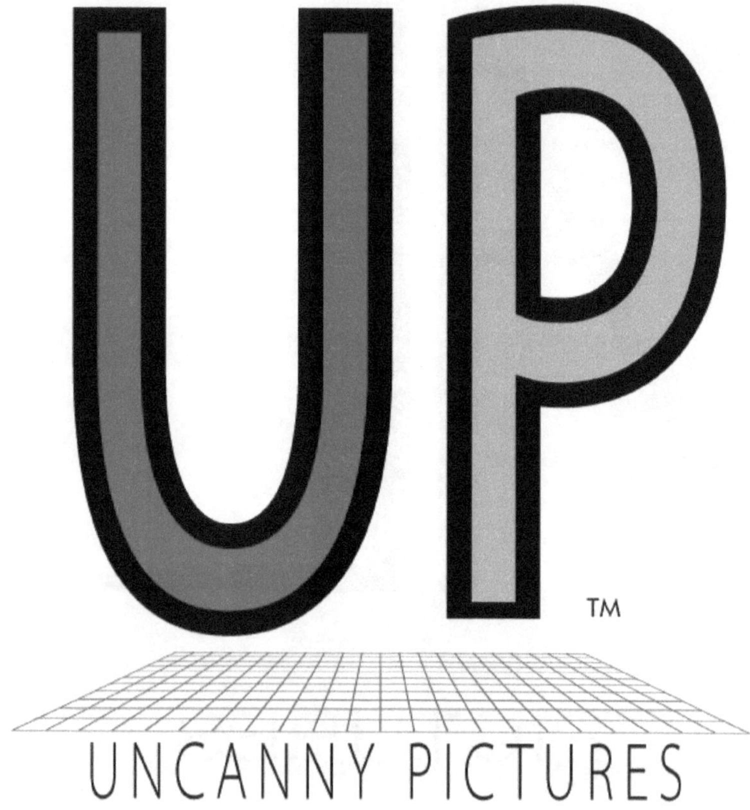

UP
TM
UNCANNY PICTURES

www.ingramcontent.com/pod-product-compliance
Lightning Source LLC
Chambersburg PA
CBHW051452250726
48655CB00001B/378